If My Couch Could Talk

SOBRIETY THROUGH PASSION AND PURPOSE

Bunny Berman, LCSW

Copyright © 2023 Bunny Berman, LCSW
All rights reserved
First Edition

Fulton Books
Meadville, PA

Published by Fulton Books 2023

ISBN 979-8-88982-454-1 (paperback)
ISBN 979-8-88982-455-8 (digital)

Printed in the United States of America

There are so many to thank, with whom this never would have been possible; My Inspirations!

First and foremost, to the woman who had a passion for people like no other, who opened her home and heart to anyone who knew her. Unfortunately, she passed away in 2018 and will never read this book, however she lives on in me everyday – Thank you mom, for being who you were and teaching me in so many ways to be who I am today;

To the individuals I have worked so closely with, especially those that have lost their lives to the disease of addiction; you are in my heart every single day and were the motivation for this book, the daily fuel that I needed to continue writing. If you only knew how important and loved you truly were; Daniel, Rich, Conor, Jeremy and Neil, and unfortunately so many others.

My children, grandchildren, family and friends, thank you each for your part in supporting me and listening all hours of the day and night,

To my amazing fiancé, John, who I'm sure never imagined what he was getting into when we met at this later stage in our lives; he is the wind beneath my wings and my motivation in each day! I love you now and forever! Thank you for always believing in me and making me a better person;

And most of all, to my dedicated partner, my couch, without whom none of this would have been possible!

Let the journey continue ---

It all began in November 2019, when she accepted the job as a clinical director of a brand-new treatment center. She had been an integral part of setting up this center, so it only seemed right that she would be the one to develop and run the clinical program. She said that she was tired of other treatment centers not really caring about their people, something about wanting to be "family centered." So when she found me in the backroom of a small furniture store and sat down, I knew this was it. I was going to somehow be part of this dream.

Three minutes later, she said, "I'll take it. It's just perfect." Perfect—me, the couch in the backroom, with all the damaged (nobody wants) pieces of furniture. Now I was wanted. I didn't even care what it was for. I was just so happy that someone wanted me. I had no idea how my life was about to change.

My adventure began as she told the saleswoman at the furniture store that she needed me ASAP. I had never felt so important! I didn't really understand what she did or why she needed me, but I was ready to go and finally belong somewhere. She paid for me and said, "It was so worth it." I have never felt "worth it" before, always just in a back room, other pieces going home with excited families, while I remained homeless, until now.

I was suddenly wrapped up in plastic, barely able to breathe, standing on end, with no awareness of where I was going, but knowing that I was on a new journey. I was thrown in the back of a truck, bounced around, and spent most of the day going from one place to another. I had plenty of time to envision where I was headed. A mansion? Maybe an ocean view? A family room? A house with kids? Will pets be on top of me? Where am I going? A new beginning—it was both exciting and scary. A new journey, much like the people that would be sitting on me, but I didn't know it then. Some fear and anxiety set in, but I figured it was better than living in the back room with other damaged pieces of furniture.

The truck stopped, and I knew I was about to be "home" for the first time in my life. I was moved into this small office, unwrapped, and the room became centered around me. Nothing had ever been centered around me. In fact, I had not even been wanted until now. So whatever she needed me for, I was all for it. Little did I know what would happen on this couch and the things I would begin to hear over the years.

Immediately people began to sit on me, saying I was perfect. A coworker of hers even asked where she got me, because she wanted one too. But my person said that I was one of a kind and there were no others left. Everyone in this office space seemed to gravitate toward me, sitting on me during a break or just talking. The reception from others was both heartwarming and frightening. I hoped I could live up to their expectations and not get worn out.

So now here I am, in a small office, painted a color called "peaceful blue." It says her name on the door with "Licensed Clinical Social Worker" under it. There are a lot of different things in this office, all made to make others comfortable. So this was it! I was beginning to understand. I am in an office with the job of making others feel better. Hmmm, I'm not sure how to do that, but as long as I am feeling so wanted, I am happy to learn. Maybe I will finally find my passion and purpose, because my past life wasn't worth much. I keep hearing that "connection, passion and purpose, and helping others" is the way to lead a healthy life and stay clean/sober. Clean? Sober? Am I in a treatment center? I have heard about them, as the news talks about the opiate epidemic being the worst ever. I don't even know what that means, but it sounds bad, especially if her whole office is dedicated to making it stop. Anything that is the focus of an entire building must be something important, and I am part of it. My curiosity has peaked, and my fear has lessened as it gets more comfortable just being here, a part of something. I do wonder how all my friends are back at the furniture store, however, I must just concentrate on me. There were so many damaged pieces there, all feeling alone and unworthy. Eventually they will find a place too, when they are just willing to surrender and allow themselves to be available to anyone who is looking. That's what I did—just allowed someone to take me, to know that it was better than being stuck and feeling that my life had no purpose.

I figured out that now I am home, and I am part of a place that wants to help others find their passion and purpose too. Well, that shouldn't be so hard. I mean, look at me, I just waited, and now I have a purpose. I'm not sure how I am going to do it, but it feels good.

Having this purpose is helping me to not dwell on the long lonely dark nights in the back of that furniture store, not focusing on being damaged and not worrying about all the people that didn't take me or talk to me, but to focus rather on all those that want me to be a part of their lives. They want to just sit in her office, saying that they feel "safe and comfortable" while sitting on me. It's happening, just by being present, I'm helping others feel safe and comfortable, and they begin to share things that I can't even believe. She explains that "whatever is said in this office stays in this office," other than the mandated reporter information that she explains to each one. "Whatever is said on this couch stays on this couch." *I get it!* I am the one who keeps the secrets, the confidential information for people to get better. The importance of me being comfortable makes sense now. Nobody shares if they are uncomfortable. It is my job to continue to provide comfort while each individual works to develop a trusting relationship with her.

People say all kinds of things that amaze and shock me. They talk about their pasts, trauma, losses, abuse, things that happened to them, things they did while using.

Using what? I wonder, but I guess those answers will come in time. It seems like an easy job I have, with a willing group of people that keep talking about "wanting to get better and make a life not worth throwing away."

Let me get this straight. She talks to people about their lives, and I make them as comfortable as possible as they share their emotions, feelings and get vulnerable. Everyone who sits on me has a story, a long story, an often-traumatic story and talks about being in pain and scared. Then they talk about taking things to their grave. I've come to realize that that means that there are things that they don't want to talk about; however, whenever someone says that, she says, "That isn't going to happen here." She then helps them talk about those very things, the things they swore they would never tell anyone. Most of them cry and then afterward say they are relieved. I guess I take their secrets to my grave, but that's okay if they feel better. She said that she won't ever tell anyone, other than the mandated things she has to report; therefore, that means that now she has everyone's secrets in her head and can't say anything. I try to tell her she can talk to me, they all do, but she doesn't do that very often, unless someone else is sitting on me. I guess she and I are a team, dedicated to helping others. She continues to talk to each person about passion and purpose—I guess this is our shared passion, and as happy as she seems to have found me, I am beyond grateful to have found her.

Honestly, having felt damaged for most of my life, these feelings are all new for me too. I wasn't made damaged. I was made just perfect, just like the people that sit on me. I was a perfectly good piece of furniture, and then suddenly, people started abusing me, eating on me, spilling things on me. Animals lay on me; some even tried to chew me up. Some kids kicked me in the feet, a cat clawed me, and little babies had their diapers changed on me. No one ever took into consideration how I felt or what that might do to me in the long term. Day after day, I was at the mercy of those that abused me, without any ability to make it stop. Then one day, I was just moved out of the house I was in. I was returned to the store where I came from, the people saying that they couldn't keep me anymore, they couldn't afford me, and I was "repossessed." I didn't know what that meant, but I surely knew that I was no longer wanted. So the store took me back, tried to clean me up, and put me in the back room with other damaged pieces, and we were all on sale. *On sale*—these words meant that no one really thought I was worth full price anymore, not worth taking the time to make sure I was clean, and not abused, not worth keeping. It was devastating. I left everything I knew and had to start over, without knowing if I wanted to or if it would truly be better. I was in that backroom for a few months, people looking at me, sitting on me, and then rejecting me. I kept trying to figure out what was wrong with me. What did I have to do to get better? To be wanted again! And then she appeared. I guess life changes when you least expect it, and whether it's better or not, you may not know until you just surrender and are willing to accept something else. I now had to connect with a new person and a new way of life, but little by little, it was becoming worth it. I would always hear her tell people, "No one changes until it's too painful to stay the same." That surely resonated with me, because losing the family I had was very painful, and I was willing to surrender and do whatever I needed to do to feel wanted again.

Most of my days were spent with people sharing their lives sitting on me, curling up on me with a blanket, crying and holding a Kleenex box tight, getting a warm smile from her and being told, "It's going to be okay. You aren't alone anymore." Now how did she know how I felt? I wasn't alone anymore. I knew she was talking to her clients, but I pretended she was talking to me. I needed to hear that. That I wasn't alone. That I was worth something. That even though I had been damaged, I could be of use to others and have a life that I could be proud of again.

The situations I faced over the next couple of years were nothing short of miraculous. A young man having been involved with substance abuse for years telling her everything, and I mean everything that he had been through, had done and all he was still struggling with. I didn't even know there was that much pain in a person, but that poor man was a mess, until he wasn't. Until he felt loved and that his life was worth it. Now I knew exactly how he felt. As he left the office that day, he gave her a hug and said, "Thank you for believing in me. That couch is magic. I have never cried so much in my life."

Magic? Me? That felt so good, I couldn't wait for the next person to come in. Myriads of people, situations, painful conversations, wonderful moments of awareness, vulnerability, willingness to listen, surrender, learning to live healthy, learning how to cope, how to become themselves and love themselves once again. As they did this, I could feel the difference in them. The young woman who wouldn't say anything for weeks was now curled up in the corner, her feet stretched out, saying she just needed to talk. The man who came in to sit on me and said, "I just need a safe place to let go of how I feel, and this couch is the safest place I've ever had." As these people faced their fears, I noticed that I didn't feel quite so damaged anymore. The past grew more distant, and the good, warm feelings began to stay. I didn't talk as badly to myself anymore, less negative thoughts, more positive thoughts, more reason to embrace all my imperfections, because they made me who I am. They made me the "magical" couch, the place people wanted to sit and share, allowing themselves to be emotional, face their fears, be honest, share their emotions yet feel safe.

Now it was time to really begin to listen to their stories. To understand what she saw in each person when she said, "I will love you until you can love yourself and then I will continue to love you." My mind flashed back to the moment in the backroom of that furniture store when she said I was perfect, when she loved me at a time when I couldn't love myself, when I felt alone and abandoned. Now I totally understood the passion and purpose in her, and I was beginning to understand the passion and purpose in me too.

When a man came in and told her of his relapse and that he was very disappointed in himself and began to cry hard, she just touched his knee and said, "It's okay, we will continue to work on it. Don't beat yourself up. That won't help. We just need to work harder on you resolving the past." I was shocked. The warm voice, the gentle approach, yet the clear message that using drugs was not okay, not in a beat-you-up way but in a caring, loving, nonjudgmental way. The man cried harder and said it was the first time he felt accepted. Yes, *accepted*! That's the word I was looking for! Accepted! Flaws and all. She said, "You aren't a product of what you have done. You are a product of who you become." Every time she talked to one of her people, I pretended she was talking to me. Maybe she was talking to me through them, I don't know, but I do know that it made me feel like I was worthy, like I was never going to be alone again, and that although there were a couple rips in me, it didn't change who I am.

There were many times when she had to call someone in because they did something wrong, relapsed, didn't follow the rules of the program, were struggling, were fighting with someone else, were disrespectful, or she had to deliver bad news. Every one of those people came in and sat on me as their safe place to deal with things that were not so safe, not so easy, and this gave them the ability to handle things that were sometimes unbearable.

So as I continue to work with her, I begin to realize that these people come in at least once a week to talk. Some come in more often. Each time, they start out by saying they are "okay" and "nothing is new." Somehow within minutes, they are digging into their pasts, exploring what she calls "core issues" and "triggers" that have led to "relapsing behaviors." I try to understand each term she uses, but I realize it doesn't matter if I understand it, just if they do.

One day, a man came walking down the hall toward her office. She and I were alone in the office, and I don't know if she realized that she was talking out loud in a very quiet voice as she saw him approach her door. "I know he has used," she said. "Darn it, he was doing so good. I wonder what happened." I guess she was talking to me, although she was looking at him. She looked sad too. As he approached the door, she said, "I know," and he came in, sat down, and began to cry. There wasn't much communication between them, like she knew these people so well. Then he described what he had done, through the emotions only a broken man knows. She rolled her chair closer to him, put her hand on his knee, and said, "It's going to be okay. Just be honest with me. I need the truth."

This man told her everything and then said, "Every time I sit on this couch, I cry. Even when I think everything is okay." She just gave him a warm smile and said, "We are a good team." She was talking about her and her client; I was listening to it as she and I. So this man now had to go to a place called a "detox center." I am not sure who was more upset, she or him, but she promised him that she would be here to help him if he chose to come back.

Two weeks later, the same man was sitting on me again, saying his only hope was to work with her again and that the couch was his safe place. It's amazing that two weeks go by and someone still remembers me and wants to sit on *me* for comfort. I guess being unconditionally loved and accepted is truly what it's all about, for both of us. I am coming to realize that we all just need someone to believe in us, and that's exactly what she does. Although she understands the relapse rate is incredibly high and so many lose their battle with this dreaded disease, there are many that move forward, become sober, and live productive lives. Believing in someone—that's the most important concept of all! When she found me and *believed* I could help others, it just began to happen. It doesn't matter if you have some damage, it doesn't matter your past, it only matters that you begin to accept and love yourself and see a vision for the future. Now that I have a passion and purpose, *I get it*!

Many of the people in this center share their pasts—having a family that no longer talks to them, family that has kicked them out. I wonder where these people went when they got kicked out. I wonder if it was like me, who was repossessed and returned to the furniture store. I know they can't be returned to where they came from, so where do they end up? Now I was curious and saddened that there are people who are just wandering around, nowhere to go and feeling unloved. I started to understand that this was because of their behaviors, but I also felt like their behaviors were the end result of their lives, not the beginning. The Band-Aid on problematic pasts, trauma, abuse. Something that took the edge off the already unbearable pain that many of them have lived. Don't the people who kick them out realize that there are past issues, things that have led to this drug use and that they need help and to be loved, not abandoned. I think it's a more complicated issue than I understand, but I know she seems to understand them all, well, most of them and is there to take off the Band-Aid and help each one heal from the inside.

There have been many moments when she teaches someone that the Band-Aid is something we need when we bleed, yet if we can heal the cut, the Band-Aid is no longer needed. She often explains core issues to each person as though they have a splinter. She shares this: "When you have a splinter, you often don't want to take it out because it hurts, and you just look at it and wonder if you should leave it in or take it out. Many times, we decide to just leave it in. Days, weeks, months go by, and skin grows over the splinter, making it less painful, yet you always know it's there. Maybe a dull ache or maybe just an awareness that something is inside that doesn't belong. Then suddenly one day, that splinter rears its head again, and now you decide it's time to just pull it out. That it might hurt more to do so, but once it's out, you feel so much better. Core issues are like this," she explains, "so hopefully on this journey of recovery, we will take out the splinters and heal from the inside, not having the pain of knowing something is there take away the ability to be feel better."

Some people can "remove their splinters" faster than others, more motivated, more able to do so. Others take time, but all I know is that in this office, each person gets the time they need and the safety they deserve. I love watching this process. It makes me feel warm and fuzzy all over again, knowing that I have played a small part in people feeling safe enough to heal.

Although there have been many positive and heartwarming moments we have shared in her office, we have had some very frightening moments in her office too. People with mental health issues that were out of control had to be placed in a "higher level of care," but she always did it with love and compassion. There was a time when she had to kick someone out of the program for their behaviors, and this young woman said some pretty horrible things to my person, but she just smiled and said, "I hope you get it together. You deserve it, and you are worth it." Not only did the young woman remain sober, but they are also close to this day, as this young woman visits the center and talks to her often. Even the ones that aren't allowed to stay feel loved and cared for most of the time. There are those that don't. They say some horrible things about the center, but she learned not to react to their words, but to just know they are people who don't feel good about themselves yet and to continue to give them words of encouragement. Acceptance, love, patience, and tolerance go a long way, even when it appears that others don't want it.

Integrity—one of her favorite words, as she describes it as, "what you do when no one is looking." Hmmm, that makes sense. So when a young man told her of the blender he stole while he was in another one of the treatment programs she ran, she was not so happy. It takes a lot to make her unhappy, where she has to give others ultimatums or more like choices in order to have another chance. Choices and chances—no, it's up to each person to make the right decision, and very often that doesn't happen for a while. In this particular instance, she found out during one of the groups she was running that this young man had stolen a blender from a local store. She was extremely upset with him and began to inquire as to what had happened.

He proudly said, "Well, I was in the self-check-out, and obviously in a self-checkout lane, stealing is expected or they wouldn't let you check out your own groceries."

She was speechless, just for a minute, because honestly she was rarely speechless, but this was one of those occasions. I think it's because she wanted to react with patience and tolerance, and right at that moment, I do believe she was battling with that. The other people in the group had mixed emotions as he shared his reasoning and what she called "distorted thinking patterns." Many thought it was inappropriate as well and helped her in confronting this irrational thinking; however, there were a couple young men that thought it was perfectly fine and said, "It was only $19.99, so what's the big deal?"

She let them know exactly what she was thinking but in a calm and reasonable manner. "It's not about the price of the item," she began to share. "It's about *integrity*."

"Integrity?" they all began to repeat it. "Hmmm, how so?" many asked.

Integrity was discussed with the passion that she always has. Then came that ultimatum. As some of the young men discussed that they used the blender to make healthy drinks (as though that made stealing it okay), she discussed the distorted thinking behind it. Distorted thinking patterns, now it began to make more sense. Distorted thinking didn't allow for rational decision-making, so now the recovery becomes even more entwined than to just not use. Distorted thinking patterns needed to be explored and rethought. Rational decision-making required forethought and a core belief that "you are worth it" and "life can be better if you do the next right thing." That learning to like life and to like loving yourself was paramount on the decision-making meter.

So back to the young man that she now calls "Blender Boy." After a long group discussion regarding integrity, distorted thinking, and irrational behavior, he was told by her that he had two choices. Remember we just discussed choices and chances. Now he could either (1) return the blender and/or pay for it or (2) he could be discharged from the program.

Wow! Here comes the reactions. He was so mad at her and said a lot of not very nice things. He was taking his distorted thinking and irrational behaviors out on her. Isn't that the way most people do things? For instance, when a police officer pulls you over for speeding, the immediate reaction is to be angry at him. When the true reaction would be to be remorseful for breaking the law. The more I hang out with her, the more I begin to understand these complicated things. Now Blender Boy has to make a decision. He has one week to decide what to do.

He began to process with her. "What am I supposed to do now?" he asked her in a very condescending tone. "Go to the store and say, 'I am a drug addict, and I stole this blender, and now I need to pay for it!'"

She was obviously more reasonable than that and said, "First of all, calm down, and we can talk about this. You can go to the store, tell the manager that you realized as you came across your receipt that you didn't pay for the blender you have and you came to take care of it."

Oh boy, did he ever give her an angry look. One week later, when she asked him what he chose to do, he angrily and very disrespectfully said, "Fine, I will go pay for it." He was taken to the store by an employee of the center that night and paid for the blender. When she asked him if he felt better about it, he adamantly said, "Nope."

This became an ongoing battle between them, until one day, he popped into her office and asked to talk. He began to cry and said that he understood her ultimatum, and he was a little happier that he did the right thing. Unfortunately, this young man lost his life to the disease of addiction after eight months clean/sober. My person had become very close to his mother through his recovery and even more so after his death. So when my person became the clinical director of this new center, she received a box in the mail a week later. She opened it in anticipation as she shared, "I rarely get packages," and as she opened it, she saw it was a brand-new *blender*. The card read, "Every center should have a blender," and it was signed, "Blender Boy's mom." Now that made her cry, which didn't happen often, but every now and then, these people would make her cry too.

Now it's time for a little background about me. I went home, brand new, many years ago, with a family. They loved me at first, I think. Then things got bad, and I had to be returned. When I was returned, it was hard to believe that anyone loved me or ever wanted me. Then one day I heard a young man say that to her as he sat on me. That he wondered why he was even born, that he was sure he wasn't wanted and that no one loved him. I was sure I found my soulmate, the one who understood me too. I was so glad to finally have someone that understood, and as the stories continued, I knew that each person in her office, had a story, and I was beginning to understand them all.

In the midst of the clients that came each week, there were so many that I could actually feel get better and become the people that they wanted to be, building a life not worth throwing away; as I saw this, I realized that I had too had built a life that I wasn't ever going to throw away. She was stuck with me forever!

I didn't understand what a recovery center was, and it took a while to realize that the people who came here all had a problem with addiction. They were all struggling with the "disease of addiction." Addiction—the fact or condition of being addicted to a particular substance, thing, or activity. There were many kinds of addiction, I learned: drugs, alcohol, gambling, food, sex, spending money, etc. This center specialized in drugs/alcohol. Each client had an addiction to either drugs, alcohol, or both. Some even had more than one addiction. They were all people with serious and painful issues, and I was honored to be a part of their healing.

One man in particular taught me the deeper meaning of acceptance as she worked with him. He had recently gotten out of a detox center and returned to the program. He had worked with her before, and she assured him that when he went to detox and if he successfully completed the detox program, she would continue the work they began prior. After about ten days, this young man returned, and she was happy to see him, relieved that he had made the decision to complete the detox program. He sat down, somewhat guarded, somewhat melancholic, as he talked about remorse, guilt, and shame—more words for me to learn the true meaning of. As he talked, with eyes that looked down at the floor, he was a bit hesitant as he shared incidents of his last relapse. She quietly listened and in a soft voice, let him know that there were better coping skills for his behaviors and that she would help him, but first he needed to make the commitment to himself. He agreed. As he continued to talk and she asked him about his passion, he was unsure. Now it was known that he was an artist and had given up his artwork when he began using drugs. He was apparently very talented, and they began to talk about getting back to his art as a way to express himself and to deal with the often painful feelings that he had internalized. She talked to him about external validation to try to heal internal pain and how that doesn't really work. Seems like many of the people addicted to substances try to validate themselves externally to fill internal voids. This young man was feeling a great deal of remorse and realized that his impulsivity was a key issue in his substance use and relapses, as was feelings of shame and guilt for his use over the years and what it did to his family.

He agreed that he had moved away from his passion for art, recognizing that when he was involved and connected to his own creativity, the craving for the substance began to dissipate. This man learned that art was his healthiest coping skill, and he began to create again, which also was a significant factor in his ongoing sobriety, making a life not worth throwing away.

There are so many stories, so many people, so much pain and lots of hectic and chaotic days. She often wonders why she does this. So many don't make it, so many leave treatment early, so many aren't ready, so much time, emotion, and energy given to others that don't even appear to care. Yet what she has come to realize is that when you do meet that one person that wants it, the one person that is grateful, the ones that stay sober, the ones that contact you years after they are done with treatment to let you know that they are still doing great, living their passion, and thank you for being a part of their journey, it all becomes worth it. Those are the moments we hang on to. Those are the moments that allow you to continue the work. Those are the moments that you have to believe in. Those are the moments when you know you are doing the right thing.

One of the most difficult things that happened to her during her work was the loss of man that she worked very closely with. He died of an overdose in the sober living residence that he lived in. He would come to the center every day, just wanting to talk and to have his lunch, as he worked as a medical assistant in the local area. This young man was going home the next day for a medical procedure for his young daughter and never made it. After us being with him until 9:30 p.m. the day before to help him plan his days at home, his anxiety got the best of him, and in an apparent effort to take the edge off, he lost his life. My person was called immediately by the other residents of the sober living residence as they knew that she worked with him. She went straight to the house at 7:00 a.m., and when she arrived, it was too late, and he had passed away. The other gentlemen in the house were all very emotional, as they felt like they lost a brother. She was one who understood that drug addicts were just people that couldn't cope, not bad people trying to get better, but sick people trying to get well. She spent the whole day with all the men who were facing this loss just as she was, and together they were able to comfort each other and share the pain of this loss. She had worked with him and spent many hours on phone sessions with family members, especially his mother, rebuilding their relationship, and everyone was very excited to see him, nervous but excited. The pain of having to talk to this mother, his wife, and other family members was almost more than she could handle. This seemed like way too high a price to pay. She wanted to quit that day; however, it was this young man's mother that made her promise that she wouldn't quit. She said her son had the best months of his life in this center and working with her and that she needed to continue to help others battle this disease. With a heavy heart, she agreed and began to use this experience as part of her work with others. This has been one of the most difficult things for her to do, yet it taught me that we can't give up. That we must find ways to handle the internal pain without using a substance. This man's death has changed her in a way that only a loss of this magnitude can do, recognizing just how tentative life can be and how important it is to help people cope in healthier ways. This man's mother and my person are close to this day, communicating often, as the pain of loss never goes away. We do find ways to move forward, forever changed. During the time of this loss, another young man had been home visiting his mother. He immediately called her, and when she answered, he said, "Momma, it's not your fault." As much as she knew her people, they knew her too! He had struggled with the disease of addiction for years, was a very bright young man, yet didn't ever feel good enough. It was another sad day when she learned a year later that he had also lost his battle with this disease. He was such an integral part of helping others. "That's how you know that the individuals who struggle with addiction," she says, "are some of the most passionate, creative, talented, sensitive, and caring individuals you could ever meet—they just don't care about themselves."

    Another gentleman, who unfortunately lost his life to this disease of addiction, had many better times through their work together. He relapsed a few times while in the treatment program, would go to detox, and then come back to her. Upon his last relapse, he had decided that he wasn't worth it and wasn't coming back to treatment. She talked with him and they made a deal of "one more time." She went on to explain that this meant that they would work together just one more time, and then if he didn't want to continue, she wouldn't ask him again. He came back and did get a number of months clean, had a relationship that he was happy in, and shared that he was less depressed than he had been in over thirty years. Unfortunately, it didn't last, and this man lost his life. It was one of her saddest days, and she again questioned why she did this work. She was the last one to speak to this man, and they had spent the better part of the day in her office, as he had relapsed and would only talk to her. He went home, and his parents called her to say that he "went on a walk" and "could she please call him, because he wouldn't answer anyone else?" They spoke for a while, and within an hour after they hung up, he passed away. My person had a difficult time, saying that "being someone's last phone call is painful." She had had this happen a few times in her career. It was this man's parents that began to comfort her and tell her that he had good days because of the work he did with her and that she can't leave this work. So she continues to work with those that are led to her.

There are numerous stories, people who continue to suffer and continue to relapse. Individuals who have built a life that they are proud of. Whether they get it their first time through treatment or it takes multiple tries, she is always there to greet each individual with a belief in their ability to stay substance free. Sometimes we have to think outside of the box, there is no "one size fits all" for recovery; however, if you are willing to take the time to get to know each individual, there is a recovery plan for anyone willing to follow it. Complacency becomes a significant issue, as it is human nature to stop doing things that are working. Why is that? I often wonder, but there is no clear-cut answer, other than we get comfortable, and when we get too comfortable, we tend to go back to our past ways, and before you know it, a relapse happens. As I have learned, a relapse happens many weeks prior to an individual actually using. Healing the shame, guilt, core issues, trauma, and past issues that have led to substance use is essential to live a clean and sober life. So many individuals have contacted her over the years, shared their successes, sometimes even their failures, but they have learned that they will always have a safe place when it comes to she and I. As for me, I now have a life that is filled with passion and purpose, and I can't believe how different it is. There are times when I do remember being in the back of the furniture store; however, looking forward is so much more meaningful than looking backward. My person says, "The front windshield is bigger than the rearview mirror for a reason."

I just hope to continue to be her partner in this quest to help others find their passion and purpose, because I finally know that I have found mine.

What I have learned in my work with her, in finding my own passion and purpose, is that the stories are endless, the emotions are high, the behaviors are often inappropriate; however, the people that maintain sobriety, that live a life not worth throwing away, that continue their recovery, surrendering and becoming open to learning about themselves and their willingness to live differently, beginning to help others, finding their passion and purpose, make it all worthwhile.

About the Author

Bunny Berman has been a licensed clinical social worker (LCSW) for over thirty years, having graduated from Michigan State University, with her bachelor's degree in psychology and a master's degree in social work. She has a passion for helping individuals, especially those with substance use disorders, to find their own passion and purpose to live sober, healthy, and productive lives.

Ms. Berman has been an integral part of developing clinical programs and takes pride in her ability to connect to people in all walks of life and seeing the world through their eyes to assist them in finding their true selves.

Ms. Berman had a dream as a young adult of creating safe therapeutic environments for others to work through the often traumatic events of their lives that have led to making unhealthy choices. It began in 1972, with her working at a day camp in Michigan when she was twelve years old and having to call the police on a child abuse case when no one else seemed to care. Realizing that there were limited resources at that time, it sparked her continued passion for developing services for people to get the help they need to live safely, whether from others or from themselves.

When not helping others or writing her next book, you will find Bunny spending time with her children, grandchildren, and fiancé, as her family is what fuels her passion.

Printed in the USA
CPSIA information can be obtained
at www.ICGtesting.com
LVHW090936270924
792207LV00002B/430